FORGIVENESS AT WORK:

Stories of the Power, Possibility, and Practice of Forgiveness in the Workplace

Deborah Welch, Ph.D.

v

Disclaimer and Terms of Use: The author and publisher have strived to be as accurate and complete as possible in the creation of this book. If an error of any kind is found please forward correct information to the author for corrections at www.storiestorenew.com.

First Printing, 2011

Cover design by Thom Welch

The back cover art includes a painting of Edith Stauffer by Alice Matzkin reprinted from the award-winning book, *The Art of Aging: Celebrating the Authentic Aging Self,* Boulder, CO: Sentient Publications, 2009. Copyright © 2009 by Richard and Alice Matzkin. Used by permission of Sentient Publications and Alice Matzkin.

Printed in the United States of America

ISBN:
ISBN-13: 978-1466485853
ISBN-10: 146648585X

ACKNOWLEDGMENTS

This book is dedicated to Edith Stauffer. I did my best to carry forward what she gave me through her extraordinary mentoring and teaching.

Also, these stories of forgiveness in the workplace would never have landed published in a book without the result of the efforts of many friends who reviewed multiple drafts, encouraged me, and kept the importance of this book alive: Thom Welch, Virginia Duncan Gilmore, Rebecca Braden Nordeman, Will Voegele, Victoria Gamber, Gail Petersen, Barb Goodwin, Gail Malay, Holly Adkins, Mark Arcuri, Sara Jarvis, Chris Voegele, Bill Voegele, Marlan Gamber, Midge Miles, Cathy Wolfe, RJ Benningham, Beth Sicora, Lee Elders, Brit Elders, Don Frick, Naomi Rose, Karen Speerstra and Ronda Harris. Thank you all deeply for your constant support.

I am also so grateful to those who offered stories, mentoring or interviews along the way, or inspired me with their writing: Parker Palmer, Ann McGee-Cooper, Michael Lindfield, Fred Luskin, Michael Stone, Howard Behar, and Andy Himes. I also thank Alice Matzkin for permission to use her beautiful painting of Edith (on the back cover). Also finally, thank you to Edith's daughter, Barbara Giles, for permission to use stories from her mother's excellent and inspiring book.

CONTENTS

INTRODUCTION

Everywhere we look on television, the Internet, and in our newspapers, we see cynicism, blame, and conflict. We can find alternative stories about courage, resilience, appreciation and trust if we look for them, but, they aren't often in the headlines.

We encounter big and little offenses and losses every day at work. However, in our difficult moments, we either get stifled or, hopefully, grow stronger from the hardships we encounter. What isn't often discussed is what it takes to go from hardship to greater courage, trust, and resilience. A key that is often operating invisibly is forgiveness. Forgiveness is defined here as *the releasing of the burden of unnecessary suffering.* Teams of researchers have discovered that forgiveness has the power to enhance our health, confidence, happiness, productivity and our relationships.[1]

Most of us know the importance of forgiveness from the most significant person to us in life. Perhaps we remember times we forgave or have been forgiven that made a tremendous difference in whether a relationship would grow or diminish. What often isn't considered is how to apply forgiveness at work. Some of us may say, "I'll practice forgiveness in my personal life and with my family –but won't invest that in work relationships – I don't have time." But think of how much time we spend at work – more than half of our waking hours. And with the stress that can build up from anger, irritation, and resentment, we end up taking that home, and it affects our health and quality of life in major ways. Also, there are so many ways the workplace is enhanced when there is a spirit of forgiveness operating. Michael

Stone, a consultant and host of the radio show "Conversations: Are We Listening?" says it so well. *"Forgiveness provides opportunities to use mistakes, failures, flaws and breakdowns of life as opportunities to awaken greater wisdom, compassion and capability in our coworkers and ourselves."* [2]

The purpose of this book is to grow our forgiveness skills in order to awaken greater wisdom, compassion, and courage in work and in life. In relationships where there is strength and caring and trust, forgiveness is always operating. It is a powerful force, but many times it is invisible because most of us don't talk about our forgiveness choices or practices. We hear about blame and retaliation much more often than we hear about forgiveness in the workplace, even though it is happening every day.

This is a book of stories because:

Storytelling is one of the most powerful

ways to learn. Stories cut right through the philosophies, language differences, abstractions and confusions and help us see important truths.

Stories can help us understand the meaning and power of forgiveness.

Reading stories of forgiveness in action can lead to a better understanding of ways we can apply forgiveness in our lives.

Stories can bring us along emotionally as well as through intellect, which can have a growth-enhancing effect.

Hearing someone else's stories can evoke our own stories. We can then begin to see a deeper truth and write a new story for ourselves.

In the following pages, you will find stories from corporate, educational, military, non-profit, and a variety of other workplace settings. Every story in this book may not be helpful or fully represent for you the awesome and mysterious power of forgiveness. Forgiveness has many faces. I hope you will keep reading and find the stories that open your heart and evoke your own story. That is all it takes. I share my own journey with forgiveness and invite you to consider your own story as you read. If even one story rings true for you, it can start a process that will help you to discover deeper truths and stronger practices. This is an opportunity to find forgiveness or integrate forgiveness practices more strongly in life and work. Stories of forgiveness say it best, so I turn to them now.

PART 1:

CHOOSING TO FORGIVE

There are many times that events in our lives are not what we wanted, not what we asked for, and not what we thought we needed. We may experience the betrayal of a co-worker, lose a job, experience a corporate merger or takeover, or lose the sale that we really needed this month. Although some suffering is unavoidable, in our hardest life moments we often feel trapped in anger or blame. Forgiveness helps us find our way to new meaning in the difficult challenges that occurred.

The following stories illustrate forgiveness during workplace hardships. In the first story, a faculty member is suddenly and unexpectedly denied tenure. In the second story, American Express corporate sales people face the pain of a lost sale. These stories help me to let go when I am challenged and to open my heart in difficult circumstances. They help me remember that sometimes it takes time to get beyond a major life challenge; and at other times I can benefit from applying forgiveness to what seems like a slow drip of disappointments that can happen in life.

CHAPTER ONE

Rising Through the Ashes – Loss of Faculty Tenure

In an economic downturn many of us struggle with organizational downsizing and job loss. This impacts not only our potential economic well being, but we can feel shock, betrayal, grief, and experience feelings of low self worth. We may begin to ask "Who am I" if I'm not this job?" This story illustrates how it is possible to let go of a long time dream, walk right through an experience of betrayal, and find a new beginning on the other side of the loss. Ann McGee-Cooper is a wise thought-leader in the field of servant leadership who regularly inspires me and thousands of others to dream great dreams. I have been privileged to have Ann's mentoring for over a decade and to learn from her work building high trust culture in organizations. This story begins with a job loss, in this case related to a loss of tenure in a university.

Valuable Lessons in Forgiveness

When I think of learning to forgive I think of one of the most painful losses of my life, how long I held on to bitterness, anger and deep emotional wounding and how my beloved spouse, Larry, taught me to let go and forgive. Here is how it unfolded.

After ten years of teaching experience, I was recruited by a Texas university to teach art education. Although I didn't feel ready, my principal urged me to accept, telling me that I was needed to recruit and mentor a different kind of teacher into the profession, ones who could make learning

engaging and fun and reach all
children no matter what learning
differences they might find limiting
their lives. I knew that there was a
major part of teaching that one
doesn't learn through being told. It
needs to come through experience
with youngsters and a stirring in
one's heart. So I founded what we
called The Experimental Arts
Program, which became a learning
laboratory for all of us.

College students would come on
Saturdays as part of their course
work to observe and interact with
kids of all ages. They designed a
magical environment that attracted
youngsters from all backgrounds to
come spend a Saturday morning in
lieu of cartoons or outdoor sports.
We made attendance voluntary to
test our ability to truly make learning
the most compelling way to spend a
Saturday   morning. The

semester was eight Saturdays and we typically had a waiting list because the classes were so popular, fun and engaging!

I recruited experienced teachers who were successful in very difficult teaching circumstances (many teaching in Dallas Independent School District) and had retained their joy for life and teaching. They become our diverse yet inspiring role models. They came as volunteers as there was no funding and when I founded the program I didn't even think to ask for this. I just wanted permission to be highly innovative in how we attracted college students to the profession of teaching, grow their skills and gave them a more meaningful way to test their interest and aptitude.

The youngsters we recruited from the start were primarily kids not doing well in school for a number of reasons. (We did this quietly and also had a good number of bright, eager youngsters who just loved the arts and creativity.) It seemed to me that it's fairly easy to teach those eager to learn. Where teaching becomes really challenging is to help those who struggle with learning, feel discouraged and therefore don't want to be in school. If we could create ways to attract these kids and help them become highly successful, we would have a winning model. And this is exactly what we did. Within three years we had visitors from around the world including the Minister of Education from Argentina, eager to learn how we fostered a learning environment where every child exhibited traits of genius and discovered a hunger for learning. It was the joy of discovering one's creativity through the arts and through intrinsic learning that triggered this transformational life change for us all.

Success and Disappointment…All in the Same Day!

The program grew and had over 5,000 youngsters actively participating by the seventh year. Meanwhile we kept applying for grants. Finally the day came when a call from New York, The JDR III Fund, announced that we had won a three-year grant with matching funds from two other foundations. And, amazingly, on the happiest day of my life, only a few hours later I was called in to be told that I had been denied tenure by a unanimous vote

of the Tenure Committee. This
meant that I couldn't accept the
grant. For to accept the funding I
had to commit to be in my teaching
position and as director of the
Experimental Arts Program through
the next three years. Yet being
denied tenure meant that I did not
have the support of my department
peers even though I had been
assured by my Chairperson and
Dean that I had full support for this
funding request.

Needless to say I was stunned! My
first thought was to learn why this
had happened. It was just a year
before that I had been told by the
previous department chair that I
would be awarded tenure without
question due to my remarkable
service and commendable teaching.
He suggested that it would be nice if
I was awarded tenure in the same
year that I also completed my

doctorate at Columbia University. I
believed him and trusted his word.
Yet now the message was reversed.
I asked for further clarification.

"Help me understand. If this vote
was unanimous or if it wasn't - I
need help to understand." The new
department chair stated three
reasons they were denying my
tenure. I was told:

1. "You've been divorced and we
don't think you're a good role model
for our students. This is a Methodist
University and we want to make sure
our teachers set the highest moral
examples." To which I responded,
"I agree that we as faculty should be
good role models. And it's true that
I've been divorced. I believe that
the bonds of marriage are sacred and

not to be broken. But there are times when growth takes us in very different directions and two people decide the marriage is no longer health-giving to either."

2. "You're seeing a counselor. We are concerned that you may not be mentally stable." I replied, "It is true that I've have sought out counseling on many occasions. My husband and I worked together in marriage counseling in an effort to heal our marriage. Then when we mutually agreed that a divorce was in the best interest of all, I worked with a counselor to learn how best to help our young son work through his feelings. And there have been other situations where I sought counseling. It's my belief that it's wise to get the best help you can find when you have irresolvable issues. As a teacher I'm committed to learning and growth. I'll be happy

to provide the names of all the counselors I've seen and sign a release so they can provide their assessment of my mental health." I promptly did this, but there was never a request for those records.

3. Then I heard the third reason they named for denying the tenure they had promised me earlier. "You have been seen crying in the halls. We see this as yet another sign of instability." I asked, "Which time?" Yes, I had wept when deaf children who were delighted to be dancing in our program came to me in tears. It seems that several of my peers who were faculty members stood off to the side and made rude, ridiculing remarks about the children, calling them f------ freaks, perhaps not realizing that the children could read lips. The children came to me in

tears and I wept with them, knowing that although I might try, I couldn't control the behavior of adults who resented the presence of disadvantaged deaf children. On another Saturday morning it was raining outside. These same professors walked through mud and then tracked it across the paintings of 3-year-old children who had laid their paintings in the hall to dry while they cleaned up their supplies at the end of class. How do you explain to small children why adults would ruin their paintings with big muddy boot prints?

Our goal was not only to provide a lab school where university students could grow their skills as teachers. It was also to bring children onto the campus who might never dare imagine that they could complete a college degree. We wanted them to grow personal dreams of attending this or another university to prepare for a life of great promise. Yet how could we ethically encourage minority and disadvantaged children to come participate in our lab school if there was a chance they would be mocked and ridiculed by disrespectful faculty? How do you explain to a child why adults would purposely damage art work they took such pride in creating? I finally explained to the children, "There is more beauty in you and we will find it again." So yes, I wept bitter tears, struggling myself to understand why any adult would target youngsters with such hurtful, disrespectful behavior. I was truly blind to the unintended consequences of my actions and had a great opportunity to begin asking the question. What am I doing or not doing that is contributing to what I don't want?

A Law Suit? Or Moving On…

There was a cruel irony to all this. This all took place in December of my seventh year of teaching. Legal counsel advised me that I already had the right to tenure and could thumb my nose at my colleagues. In other words, once an associate professor teaches even one day into their seventh year, they have tenure automatically. Apparently my colleagues were unaware of this information. However, my purpose in teaching was to attract the best and brightest college students to prepare as teachers. And to do so, I believed having a lab school was essential. I realized that I couldn't protect so many youngsters from a few resentful adults. And ethically, I couldn't risk inviting children to the university campus and where they might be insulted and abused by jealous peers. This would reinforce their fear that they didn't belong on a college campus, the opposite of what we hoped to create for them.

This was one of the most painful losses of my life. I had worked two full-time jobs for seven years while going back to school full-time to earn two advanced degrees. The dream was to win funding so we could take this teacher preparation program to new heights of excellence. We had achieved recognition by another excellent Texas University and the Minister of Education for Argentina who had come to visit our program and learn how we were achieving such extraordinary results. We had earned recognition and commendation from several prestigious educational groups. I struggled to understand how all this could come tumbling down by a decision that I hadn't seen coming.

Looking back I now realize that it was like God saying "you are needed elsewhere." And that is what brought me to consulting in corporations. If something so cataclysmic had not happened, I'd still because I was so deeply committed. Yet there was another calling for me to discover: teaching creativity and servant leadership in the corporate world.

But at the time I didn't let go right away. Years had passed yet I still was not able to pass by the Arts School without tremendous emotional pain. At one point my husband Larry said, "How long are

you going to carry this grievance?"
…and I replied angrily, "Maybe
forever!"   He gently added, "Don't
you realize that you are only hurting
yourself.   It's over.   Put it behind
you." And he was right. You can be
angry forever; but it only poisons
your spirit.   It was a deeply painful
lesson in so many ways.

I did find my way back from the
anger over time.   When I was ready
and needed to find a way, people
seemed to magically show up in my
life.   I once was seated on a flight to
New York next to Federal Judge
Mary Conway Kohler.   She became a
mentor.   She said to me "You're
wasting your energy in your
fear…the world needs your genius."

Turning Problems into Opportunity

Later, I could look back and ask myself "How could this problem have been an opportunity?" The gift of my lifetime is that we never got funded. I now see that at least two great gifts came out of this:

First, I learned I could do anything without funding simply by finding the synergy in balancing needs and resources.

Second, I learned to match needs with needs. Then you have dignity. It's harder, but it's more sustainable. For example, someone needs the arts program and has a building and room for an arts program. We needed a lab school where college students could learn the art of teaching youngsters from many backgrounds with a wide range of needs. Youth detention centers, schools for the deaf, hospitals with children's psychiatric centers, inner city community centers, private schools…there were 13 organizations in Dallas where we established lab schools. We provided the faculty supervision, student teachers and creative curriculum. By bringing these two resources/needs together we discovered that we didn't need to have outside funding, just the generous gifts of time and talents by many, many incredibly dedicated volunteers.

The Courage to Ask: "What Was My Role in What Happened?"

In so many ways I can now use what I learned. Instead of seeing the experience as "How could I have let that tragic loss happen?" I view it all as a valuable preparation for what was coming next. It gave me the life experience to prepare for this moment. By reflecting with an open heart and sincere curiosity, we can learn a great deal from the past. And by inviting these lessons to enrich our futures, we can replace bitterness and resentment with gratitude and learning to assume good will.

None of us are perfect and all of us harbor bias and judgment. This painful loss taught me so much and made me a stronger, less judgmental, more reflective person. How can I take what I learned and become even more effective in our work with corporate and community leaders in the spirit of servant leadership? What I experienced launched me into a future so rich with possibility. But I could only discover the gifts by releasing my anger and hurt. I had to stop casting myself as an innocent victim. I had to find the strength to realize that all my seeming successes and the media attention that brought may have triggered polarization. I had not asked for help from my colleagues, knowing I had no money to offer. And as a result, they didn't feel a part of the wonderful program growing so profoundly each year. Some of their children participated and often on scholarship. Yet I had not had the courage to go find ways to ask for their support. Maybe they would have joined in, maybe not. But I learned a very valuable lesson. People support what they help to create. And if you don't engage those close around, you may just create a deep resentment that sucks energy reactively. It was a valuable and costly political lesson that still serves me well. Dr. Jean Houston calls this sacred wounding. And indeed it is!

Ann shares so many important life lessons that came out of a very difficult experience and the first one I would like to highlight is her process of forgiveness. She says, "What I experienced launched me into a future so rich with possibility, but I could only discover the gifts by releasing my anger and hurt." The work to move through the wounding experience is important. Ann couldn't skim over the very real suffering from a sacred wound. She had to give herself time to heal. When her husband Larry first reminded her that "a lack of forgiveness poisons your spirit," Ann didn't try to force herself to forgive too early. She took the time she needed to grieve the loss. This is something that many times we can try to skim over or ignore, and then   wonder why the old pain or pattern keeps resurfacing. By accepting that she was not yet ready to forgive, she took a step toward accepting right where she was in the process of forgiveness. She was able to grieve, face her fears and suffering, and then when ready ---she let go.

I don't know everything Larry did when he hard Ann express that she was not yet ready to forgive, but if he was anything like those who have helped me in times like these - he didn't just introduce the idea of forgiveness, perhaps he also listened to her with acceptance, patience and love. This is a fine balance that we have to learn in forgiveness work. If we skim over the grief process we don't really heal. And it is much more difficult to take on new dreams. If we dwell in suffering too long our growth is also stunted. An attitude of acceptance of ourselves can help us cooperate with a natural healing process.

We find our way not by pushing to forgive, but by asking ourselves good questions about our suffering. Self awareness and acceptance will bring us through to the other side of the pain if we are willing.

Ann expresses so beautifully so many transformational lessons that came out of this painful experience. It can be helpful to ask ourselves the questions Ann asked herself. "What could be good about this? How could this problem be an opportunity?" Perhaps Ann never would have wished for this painful experience, but later she can look back and see how it made her stronger, the skills she learned through the whole experience, the depth she has in her own character now which helps her to support other leaders dealing with suffering and loss. She emerged more compassionate and wise and able to give to others in ways probably not possible prior to the loss.

As I reflect on Ann's story, one of the things I value is that she didn't define herself by anyone else's view of her competencies, even when her career seemed to shatter. She stayed true to herself and she asked questions of everyone involved and continued to try to learn from the experience. Then when she was ready to let go, she chose not to cast herself as an innocent victim. She took the advice from a synchronous encounter to not waste energy in fear and to have the courage to forgive. And as her mentor, Robert Greenleaf said:

> One must have an attitude toward loss and being lost, a view of oneself in which powerful symbols like *burned dissolved, broken off* – however their impact is seen to be – do not appear as senseless or destructive.

Rather the losses they

suggest are seen as opening the way
for creative acts, for the receiving of
priceless gifts. Loss, every loss the
mind of man can conceive of,
creates a vacuum into which will
come (if allowed) something new
and fresh and beautiful, something
unforeseen. ...Loss by itself is not
tragic. What is tragic is the failure to
grasp the opportunity which loss
presents. [4]

Ann often reminds me to ask myself the
question, "How can this crisis actually be
an opportunity?" New life and new
possibilities emerge from the ashes of our
most difficult times. The automatic
reaction many of us have when we
experience a job loss, the loss of tenure as
an educator, or even the loss of a sale as a
sales person, is to hold on and grip tighter
to our unmet expectations. Yet,
forgiveness means that we find a way

through. We begin to ask ourselves questions and look at things through the lens of a greater meaning than we can yet see. And when we find new meaning in old events, it is a sign that true forgiveness has happened.

CHAPTER TWO

The Hurt Stops with Me – Forgiveness at American Express Corporation

Now that we have looked at how forgiveness helps us find our way through difficult workplace losses, I turn now to consider a story that speaks about how forgiveness education can happen. I can't think of anyone who has devoted more of his life to educating people around the world on the skill of forgiveness than Dr. Fred Luskin. His story begins in 1995 when he completed his dissertation on forgiveness and received a large grant to replicate the research which became the Stanford Forgiveness Project. He says, "When we were recruiting participants, we begged people to pay attention to the project and nobody was interested. We sent out a message 'Stanford Forgiveness Project looking for volunteers for a study on forgiveness'. We called all local media. One person was finally willing to do a story on us. But first the reporter asked, 'Why should we do a story on forgiveness. What's the deal here?' I said, 'Do an experiment for me. Go around the newsroom and ask if anybody has a grudge with anybody else.' He hung up and called me back three minutes later and said 'Fred, everyone hates each other.' And I said, 'That's why we want to do a study on forgiveness.'"[5]

That newsman did an in-depth 70 second piece on television which helped Stanford recruit so many participants that it turned into the largest forgiveness project ever. But Fred never forgets the roots of his work.

This is all about the fact that I was miserable because I couldn't forgive.

And I never want to lose sight of the absolute human suffering that was at the core of my experience. I go around the country now and I train lots of people and I'm "Dr. so and so" and I work at Stanford. And it's only secondarily about that. …it IS about the cost of being caught in one's own pain from suffering we can't handle. …What I did come to understand is that all the strategies I tried to use previous to forgiveness had failed me. They are the strategies we see most commonly; they are the strategies of bitterness, resentment, despair, self righteousness, self pity, a sense that the world isn't as good or as kind as we'd like it to be. These are the strategies we employ to deal with the fact that life is capricious and difficult at times and that other people fail at being good to us. …So we have these strategies and a kind of harshness. …Whatever the unkindness is; forgiveness means

the hurt and unkindness stops with
me. And that is a radical notion.

One of the best researched examples is a
study at American Express. Fred Luskin
and his team provided a one-day training
with sales people to increase emotional
competence and sales ability. They call it
learning to *navigate the world with flexibility and
grace.* The focus is on emotional
competence including practicing
forgiveness on whatever comes up day to
day. "If there is traffic ...forgive that. ...Feel
better now - then worry about what
happened in the past if you still need to."
Sales staff may, for example, have a
challenge facing multiple rejections and
expecting calls that never come through.
They learn to open their hearts regardless
of whether calls are returned or not.
Participants learn to manage stress and to
align their thoughts, emotions and
behaviors, and they examine areas for their

own growth. We tend to think of forgiveness only for very painful breaches of trust or for when deep damage has been done. But in this program, forgiveness principles help sales people let go of the negative feelings when a sale doesn't come through or when a boss irritates them.

Remarkably, at the end of the year the American Express advisors who participated in this project demonstrated a 60% to 400% improvement in productivity over their peers, along with a 25% reduction in stress and an increased in positive mood. Imagine the reduction of suffering, the lowered time and energy spent on health care, and the energy available for greater use in a challenging workplace. Fred explains, "The capacity to keep one's heart open even when things turn out badly, even when we fail -- is an important capacity."

Fred explains the difference between forgiveness and coping.

Forgiveness is the decision that 'the hurt stops with me.' It is the commitment to release and stop the cycle of pain. …It could be your computer crashes, or your colleague screws up, or somebody cancels an order and a sale falls through. Whatever the suffering or disappointment you may encounter, each of us should consider if the strategy we are using is working for us. The old strategies of anger, reciprocal response, withdrawal, complaining, bitter jokes, feeling sorry for ourselves, etc. don't bring us peace. ..When we face suffering there are two main avenues out of that – coping or forgiveness. Coping is when we say I will simply 'get through this with the passage of time.' We move forward with bitterness, and some degree of 'I just gotta battle through this.' This is basic coping as we stay with the old strategies. This is in contrast to forgiveness. With forgiveness you don't just cope, you learn to become aware of new forgiveness skills that you can bring to bear now, and to future problems. You can cultivate forgiveness which will give you a greater efficacy and likelihood for handling the next thing that comes down the pike more skillfully.

Fred gives an example from a workshop in which someone shared about being lied to at work. It had been two years since this event but his adrenalin was all charged up against this enemy. Fred's coaching was to ask the question, "Can you let go of your attachment to this and tell me the story without the adrenalin?" Take a deep breath and quiet down your mind. Don't let adrenalin determine   your story.   It is like unclenching a fist. Our way of thinking and being tends to constrict around a wound. It's tighter and narrows around the wound. With forgiveness it tends to open back up; like a fist that was clenched and then opens."

Forgiveness means *the hurt stops with me* according to Fred Luskin's compelling definition. Imagine if we all stopped carrying forward the broken patterns from the past in our workplace and politics? Imagine if we strengthened the best of what has been passed along to us and just let go of the rest. Sometimes forgiveness is only associated with gut wrenching pain. But that does a disservice to the importance of forgiving small things and the power of building our forgiveness muscles.

Fred Luskin and his team work with

thousands of college students, corporate leaders, lawyers, doctors, hospital staff, church leaders, and have even gone into the midst of conflict in Northern Ireland to help heal the wounds of war. I have had the honor of interviewing dozens of extraordinary, caring, and uplifting thought leaders. But when I spoke with Fred, I realized that I had never left any other interview knowing more about myself, rather than just learning about the remarkable person I had interviewed. He concluded the interview by saying,

These are human questions that have been with us forever and every one of us struggles with them. After so many years of teaching forgiveness it's so obvious to me that we don't have to stay stuck if we don't want to. Forgiveness is one of the conditions of happiness.

PART 2:

PREPARING THE WAY FOR FORGIVENESS

There are many times we come to a forgiveness process experiencing rage or deep grief. There are plenty of reasons for this. We find many of our organizations failing financially and/or ethically. People can seem to be used up and discarded in an organizational system, or difficult politics can result in someone feeling thrown under the bus. There are rivalries, lynch mobs, stealing of ideas, incivility, a lack of jobs available when they are needed, and more. This may lead us to feel difficult emotions we don't want to feel. We believe there is just no time for forgiveness work, or we may not even know that we need to forgive. Wherever you find yourself today, the following two stories may be useful to you. They have helped me with understanding how to prepare the way for forgiveness. In the first story, a young graduate with his freshly-earned architecture degree is challenged with a difficult job search. In the second story a facilitator tells a story of helping a minister who seems stuck in her work to enter a more forgiving state of mind.

CHAPTER THREE

A Moment for Renewal – The Grueling Job Search

This is a story told by my brother, Will, who graduated with a degree in architecture, but then found himself in a painful job search. His story teaches me many things. One is that sometimes when we need forgiveness most, we may not realize our need.

I grew up in a performance-oriented environment. I learned to always do the right thing and the responsible thing. This wasn't necessarily bad. I learned a lot of important lessons about honesty and responsibility. But inherent in all of this was the concept that if something could not be accomplished, then one simply needed to employ the right tools, make the right call, take another step, work harder, try harder. Again, conceptually this isn't a harmful approach to problem solving, as patience and perseverance are hallmarks of success. That is, unless the process leads to self-doubt, criticism, self-condemnation and not being good enough – the idea is that if something isn't being accomplished, it must be your fault because you're not doing something right.

This was demonstrated most clearly in my life when I graduated from college. I had spent four years getting the system down and learning to do what was required to be successful – to get good grades and cause things to happen the way I wanted. I had been president of my fraternity and experienced success in what felt like every aspect of my life.

So, getting a good job right out of college would be a no brainer – right?

I was on a mission to find my first job as an architect, and after traveling literally across the country in search of someone to hire me without success, I decided to return to my college town and search a little closer to home. I had such incredible expectations and placed so much pressure on myself that every unsuccessful interview, every unreturned call was followed by a self-inflicted blow to my self worth, self confidence and self esteem. I tried every tool I had. I worked feverishly. I interviewed with anyone who would meet with me, and I offered to work for free for one week if they would just give me the chance. But there were no offers. I hated myself, and I hated every architect who wouldn't give me a foot in the door. I was out of ideas and out of architects to call.

I was living at my fraternity house that summer with some great friends who were there for summer school. They couldn't figure out what was wrong with me. I wasn't much fun to be around. I could have been having a blast while patiently looking for a job. But I was miserable. One hot afternoon, with nothing to do but cut the grass, I took a break to pick up the mail. I found a letter from my girlfriend. She knew how despondent I had been. Her letter to me consisted mostly of quotes that inspired her about love and forgiveness.

I remember sitting on the porch and thinking to myself, "What am I doing? If I could really control all of this – if I could really choose what was happening – would I have chosen this outcome?" The obvious answer was, of course not! So maybe I really wasn't in control of these circumstances after all. Maybe I really wasn't such a bad person as I was inclined to believe. With all my tools, nothing I could do, including offering to work for free, was leading to what I was so desperately focused on achieving.

I remember sitting there and deciding that it was all ok – and that I was ok. I forgave myself, and I forgave all of the architects who would not offer me a job. I felt an incredible weight lifted from me.

I got up to finish the grass and just after starting the lawn mower, one of

my friends living in the house
signaled to me that I had a phone
call. It was my first job offer,
literally minutes after I had forgiven
myself and everyone around me. It
was like the floodgates were just
waiting to open…waiting for me to
get out of the way.

Will's story reminds me of the choice I
have in each moment. If I am holding
myself back from enjoying life, often there
is something under the surface. Sometimes
my pain is so well hidden or ignored for so
long I am numb. I may not even realize I
have been so critical of myself and others.
In just one moment of awareness, things
can get easier if I make a new choice. It
can be in response to a poem, a quote, a
letter, an email, a call from a loved one, a
spiritual verse, a moment sitting and
noticing the brilliant, green grass. Any one
of these things can help me prepare the

way for a spirit of forgiveness. I have seen time and again that a new awareness can come from taking just one moment to shift perspective.

When we unburden ourselves from unnecessary suffering, we are free to use our energy for more important uses. We open up to use more of our gifts and strengths. Sometimes the sense of inner peace and an open heart is the main result. If nothing else were to happen other than feeling that a weight has been lifted, that is worthwhile and valuable. In the case of Will's story, he went on to use his degree to become a developer in charge of billion-dollar projects. Additionally, he is a gifted musician and songwriter.

When I reflect on Will's account, I notice how the phone rings right after he has a change of heart. I am always surprised and in awe when I hear synchronicity stories.

And at the same time, I realize that I have seen this sort of synchronicity often enough during forgiveness work to expect some happy surprises. It isn't easy work to forgive. It doesn't often happen so quickly for me. But it does usually have happy outcomes. The first step is to slow down, relax, and do what we can to open our minds and hearts. Thus, we prepare the way.[6]

CHAPTER FOUR

Starting With Little Things – A Minister's Leadership Challenge

This next story is about helping others to prepare for forgiveness, and it comes from one of the finest facilitators I have ever known. I met Dr. Edith Stauffer in 1978, when she was in her 60s. She mentored me for thirty years and traveled around the world teaching about unconditional love and forgiveness until she was in her 90s. She has been a wisdom figure for many, many people and studied with Italian psychologist Roberto Assagioi. Alice Matzkin's painting of Edith reprinted from the dual award winning book, *The Art of Aging: Celebrating the Authentic Aging Self* can be found on the back cover of this book. [7]

Edith was only about 5 feet tall, but she had the biggest presence of anyone I had ever met. Here is one of her stories.

A young woman minister was assigned to her first pastorate. In a workshop on forgiveness, this minister brought up eight or ten expectations and demands the church people had put upon her which she could not fulfill. Each demand was related to her being a woman. She felt hostile and angry. I encouraged her to get her anger out. Then I took the simplest item on her list, hoping she could forgive it and then use the energy generated to forgive more complex situations. She could not forgive even the simplest incident.

This was years ago, before I was skilled in teaching people how to use love. But I knew that gratitude was one of the fastest ways of elevating consciousness, so I asked group members to say aloud what they were grateful for. I encouraged them to speak spontaneously, regardless of who else might be speaking. They named health, friends, love, beauty, humor, family, children and many other things. I could feel the energy of the group elevating.

Then I asked the minister, who had named many things for which she was grateful, if she was ready to forgive the people in her congregation. We started with the simplest item and continued till she had forgiven everyone involved. It was in this experience that I learned one cannot heal a situation on the same level at which it was created. If we react angrily to something that was done to us, it cannot be forgiven while we are at that level of

consciousness of anger or
resentment." [8]

I learn from Edith's story that forgiveness
begins when we open our hearts even if
only very slightly. Gratitude is one way I
know to do this. One of my morning
practices is to keep a gratitude journal. I
can fall into cynicism and so easily forget
those things in my life that are valuable and
precious in each and every day. The
gratitude journal puts everything back in
perspective. Bringing up a topic for
forgiveness can feel stressful. The issue for
which I want to forgive may be something
around which I am currently in an attack or
defend mode. It is practically impossible
to forgive when anger or adrenalin is
pumping through your body. As Fred
Luskin explains, "If we are not calm the
part of the brain that opens up to the
positive emotional state shuts down and
there is not much you can do." [9] Stress

chemicals limit the amount of blood flow available to think, and we get trapped in a fight or flight response. A quick way to reverse the stress response is to start with two or three deep cleansing breaths. Simply focus on breathing. Athletes, professional singers, and dancers learn to breathe deeply to gain physical and emotional power.[10] Studies have found that for 80% of people, forgiveness happens in a meditative, calm state. [11]

So how do we begin to reach a more relaxed state? Buddhists actually have a name for the distracted, worried state which often arises when life doesn't meet up to our expectations. They call it *monkey mind*. Sometimes reaching a relaxed state is like tuning a radio dial just slightly – away from the static and monkey mind thoughts – toward harmonious thoughts and feelings. This requires practice. Every time I choose to be calm, I prepare the way for forgiveness and grow my capabilities

Although it sounds so simple to take a moment to reflect and enter a spirit of forgiveness, most of my experiences with forgiveness have not been quick or easy. Many times I approach forgiveness with difficult emotions that I can't shake or with a busy mind that won't let go of worry or irritation.   Victor Frankl said "Between stimulus and response there is a space...and in that space lies our choices and our freedom." [12]

I can always ask myself, "What is it in this space I have right now between me and the pain?"

I find that sometimes I can open my heart through thinking of things I'm grateful for, and other times my heart opens more if I accept whatever it is that I am feeling – even if it is anger, or pain or something I don't want to feel. There are many different paths to this state where your mind is calm, where you can remember that life is more than this pain or agitation or distraction. It just takes finding one method for attaining calm or gratitude that works well for you as an individual, and then you can use that to prepare the way for forgiveness. Forgiveness expert Fred Luskin puts it like this. "Think of someone you absolutely love, sometime you felt you were truly of service. Think of something beautiful around you. Hold that image in your mind. That is enough. Your body calms and your mind gets free."[13]   Or as Edith Stauffer would say, "There is a place in you where nothing disturbs your peace. With forgiveness, you rest in that place."[14]

PART 3:

ESSENTIAL FOR THE GIFT OF FORGIVENESS

One of the most important forms of forgiveness, self forgiveness, is often the one we neglect the most. A project failed and we can't stop blaming ourselves. Or we keep self-sabotaging and derailing ourselves and are not really sure why. We may unintentionally betray a confidence with the slip of an email to the wrong address. We may have been unfair to an employee or neglected to credit someone who deserved it. It could be big failures or little ways that we let a slow drip of self criticism build up in our lives. Whatever the issue, large or small, learning to forgive ourselves is a key to learning from our errors and to recover with strength, confidence and resiliency. Also, it is difficult to forgive others when we can't forgive ourselves. In the next chapters we explore elements of self forgiveness through the story of a well known author and architect, and then I share one of my own stories from a time that I almost derailed my career due to a lack of self-forgiveness.

CHAPTER FIVE

Self Forgiveness Failure and the Inessential

To begin to explore elements of self forgiveness, I want to share a few quotes from history makers Buckminster Fuller and J.K. Rowling.

Buckminster Fuller is best known for inventing the geodesic dome, but many people don't know that when his first child died, he suffered from a lot of guilt. During that time in his life Bucky, as many called him, described himself as "discredited, bankrupt, jobless and on the verge of suicide." He actually stayed in silence and rarely spoke at all for two entire years. After spending enough time in silence a pivotal thought came to him. "It struck me that my life belonged not to myself but to the universe...I chose to embark on an experiment to discover what the little, penniless, unknown individual might be able to do effectively on behalf of humanity." He had many concerns about the ecosystem and went to work on these problems. Over the next fifty-four years he developed projects like the geodesic dome, was awarded 25 patents, authored 28 books, received 47 honorary doctorates, and dozens of architectural design awards. [15]

I don't know what all happened in those two years of silence from which Buckminster Fuller found his way from self-diminishment to catapult forward into amazing good work for the world. But his opening to wonder what a "little, penniless unknown individual might do on behalf of humanity" reminds me that in any moment there is an option to choose once accept things exactly as they are, no matter how dark things seem and choose to live my purpose. Even at a time when life is not at all what I expected there is still an opportunity to look with awe and wonder at what could be possible. I know that we all have those bottom places in life. These can be the starting place for more meaning and purpose than we have ever before experienced.

And then J. K. Rowling, author of the Harry Potter series, speaks about a pivotal experience as well, as she discusses hitting a bottom and reflecting on experiences of failure in a speech to college graduates. She says:

> Ultimately, we all have to decide for ourselves what constitutes failure, but the world is quite eager to give you a set of criteria if you let it. By any conventional measure seven years after my graduation day I had failed on an epic scale. A short-lived

marriage had imploded, and I was jobless, a lone parent, and as poor as it is possible to be, without being homeless. The fears I had had for my self had come to pass. I was the biggest failure I knew. Now, I am not going to tell you that failure is fun. That period of my life was a dark one, and I had no idea that there was going to be what the press has since represented as a kind of fairy tale resolution. I had no idea how far the tunnel extended, and for a long time, any light at the end of it was a hope rather than a reality. So why do I talk about the benefits of failure? It is simply because failure meant a stripping away of the inessential. I stopped pretending to myself that I was anything other than what I was, and began to direct all my energy into finishing the only work that mattered to me. Had I really succeeded at anything else, I

might never have found the
determination to succeed in the one
arena I believed I truly belonged. I
was set free, because my greatest fear
had already been realized, and I was
still alive, and so rock bottom
became the solid foundation on
which I rebuilt my life. ...Failure
gave me an inner security that I had
never attained by passing
examinations. ... Life is difficult,
and complicated, and beyond
anyone's total control. And the
humility to know that will enable you
to survive its vicissitudes. [16]

"Failure can strip away what is inessential"
and "rock bottom can become the solid
foundation on which we rebuild our lives."
These words are deeply true. Making a
new beginning in the way Rowling and
Fuller did is a powerful way to discover
what matters most and to connect with
what is most meaningful and our sense of
purpose. There is   something that has to

happen inside for many of us, though, in order to move from this bottom place toward a new sense of purpose and inner security. That is where forgiveness often must comes in. Forgiveness expert Fred Luskin, from The Stanford Forgiveness Project, says, "We only need forgiveness when life doesn't meet our expectations and we get stuck wanting things to be different than they are. That is when we suffer."

We shouldn't underestimate what it takes to release our expectations and demands as to who we think we should be or how we think things should be. Many times instead of experiencing this movement to our deep sense of purpose we become paralyzed instead. Lee Taft, an expert on apology in the workplace tells about what happens in the wake of physician's errors. Often our doctors become "paralyzed by shame" after agonizing over "the harm caused, the loss

of patients' trust, the loss of their
colleagues' respect, their diminished self-
confidence, and the potential effects of the
error on their career." In the midst of
angst, the physician unintentionally begins
to push the patient away. More errors
begins to occur leading to more shame, and
this can lead to a downward spiral of
burnout and risk for addiction and even
suicide. [17]

I share this because there are depths of
becoming closed in, frozen, or paralyzed
that happen for all of us -- no matter how
intelligent and accomplished we may be.
Although we are not all in a position to
make life and death decisions day to day,
we all make errors, and we must learn how
to get off of the slippery slope of self-
condemnation in our most difficult times.

CHAPTER SIX

Moving from Insight to Habit - My Journey

Sometimes we are not aware that we are in a condition of self-criticism, or that we need forgiveness of ourselves or others. It often happens that small incidents build up, and we don't realize that we have built a case against ourselves.

Here is a personal example: While writing this chapter, my inner critic seemed to be perched on my shoulder with a constant reminder of how little I know about forgiveness. My inner editor says, "Yes, I have had amazing experiences with forgiveness that I want to share, but it feels like a drop in the bucket. I facilitate and coach others on self forgiveness, but not as much as I could. I practice, but not enough." The times I meet a situation with a lack of self -forgiveness are more glaring now that I am writing on this topic. "What do I know anyway?" The more I write on self- forgiveness the more I have had to confront all the times I have been unkind to myself. Who do I think I am to write on self forgiveness anyway?

I have been through this guilt invoking self-attack enough times to know intellectually that it is the wrong direction and is never helpful. Every time I raise my self awareness it is easy to become self critical. It is easy to wonder, "Why didn't I see that earlier, do that sooner, or better?" However I try to just get back on track more quickly, forgive more often, and to always remember that as Geneen Roth says, "In the condition of self-criticism the full truth doesn't reveal itself." Moving this understanding from my head to my heart, feeling deep peace in my own skin, is more than an intellectual exercise.

This may sound simple, but takes a real commitment to make this movement toward self-compassion. Self-forgiveness author Thom Rutledge says it well, "We live in an environment that teaches us self-condemnation. Our feelings store up and become hardened. The key to unblocking this is finding the route to self-compassion. Insight alone is not enough."
18

Personal rituals are one short and simple way to demonstrate an act of intention and create repetition. They help us build habits to sustain what matters most. Some rituals are spiritual practices such as praying for the person who has hurt or angered us, or by going to a place of worship and doing a forgiveness meditation. Another is to write whatever you want to let go of on a piece of paper and then burn the paper, which symbolizes letting go. Finally, there are many great books that provide a series of steps to forgiveness that can be done with a coach, or counselor, or in a journaling process.[19]

I learned a little process that I have done so many times that it has become a ritual. It is an automatic way for me to move to a deeper sense of my own purpose, to a little more self-compassion, and to lighten up the grip I am holding on the way I want life to be. Whenever I have pain in my life I go to my forgiveness journal and I remember what I learned from Edith Stauffer. I would drive two hours to see her each month. She would greet me with a cup of tea and guide me to freedom from patterns of pain that I had carried for years. Truly, ways that I self-sabotaged or derailed myself vanished through a little forgiveness ritual she did with me. I stopped overeating patterns, I found a loving life partner, and I became more successful and happy in my work. It strengthened me when I found myself in increasingly difficult leadership roles at work. But most important of all, I felt a sense of deep inner peace. And that deep sense of peace led to experiencing more thriving in life.

I have used these steps so often they have become automatic. Recently, I realized my husband, Thom, uses them automatically too. The ritual is simple, making it is easy to write or recite aloud.

It starts with finding a way to express my feelings and fears related to whatever it is I would like to forgive. The willingness to face an emotion or a fear that has been lingering below the surface can begin a healing process. This is especially true if I can get underneath my victim story to naming the bottom line feeling or fear in a few words. The feeling could be

disappointment, fear that I am not enough,
sadness that I didn't measure up in the way
I wish I could have, or some other feeling.
If I can take a moment to accept what it is
I am experiencing without judging the
feeling, it will often lighten up.

Right after identifying a word for the
feeling that seems to be triggering my
suffering or negative self talk, I then move
to a second statement. I express in a word
or two a positive intent that I wish could be
met. This is something I wished for
instead of my experience, an uncovering of
my truest hope, or my essential deepest
need. Sometimes I have to do this more
than once. It is helpful to go deeper than
my usual, "this is the least that could
happen" kind of response. I try to express
what I preferred in a way that opens my
heart when I imagine things happening
differently.

Here is one example of the hundreds of
times I have used this little ritual Edith

gave me to let go of suffering and forgive myself.

1. I want to forgive myself for diminishing myself. I have been feeling incompetent. I have been telling myself I am not good enough.

2. I prefer I could somehow release this perfectionism.

I prefer to remember that I am writing about forgiveness to learn more about it myself.

I prefer to remember I am developing my own habits of forgiveness through practice.

I prefer that I feel good knowing I have been as true to this project as I know how to be.

I am learning how to pass along the gift my mentor, Edith, gave me.

By naming my positive intent or preferences, I become aware of my true commitment and my sense of purpose in the situation. Just for a moment I begin to consider that everything is not reliant on how I was seeing things in the grip of fear or painful feelings. When the words I say feel wholehearted, that is a sign that I am closest to a true intent. I begin to realize there are opportunities to fulfill the hope or preference starting right now.

Then there is one last final part to Edith's ritual.

3. I cancel my expectations that I should be perfect and send myself love exactly as I am."

Edith would explain that the word *forgiveness* literally means *cancel* in the Aramaic language. I can cancel all the ways I hold onto things and see beyond my limited perspective. Journaling this way helps me to let go of unmet expectations and to remind myself that life is what it is, and within that I still have choices. I can choose to cross over from fear to love, or from anxiety to peace. I begin to connect with a sense of gratitude. And as I find myself writing, "I am grateful for Edith and everyone whose shoulders I stand on. I am grateful I don't have to try to be perfect, I just want to practice crossing back over from fear to love more easily, more often. This is the essence of forgiveness, to drop or cancel unnecessary suffering and have energy freed up to invest in what matters."

That little ritual may seem simple, but I find that the greatest things in life *are* simple. A key is to find whatever ritual you can do that can become a habit that helps you to dump unnecessary suffering and remember who you are and what you really are about in your life.

Martha Graham, the famous choreographer, described opening up to purpose and possibility in a way that inspires me. She said, "There is a vitality, an energy, that is translated through you into action. And because there is only one of you in all of time, this expression is unique. And if you block it, it will never exist through any other medium and it will be lost. The world will not have it. It is not your business to determine how good it is nor how valuable nor how it compares with other expressions. It is your business to keep it yours clearly and directly, to keep the channel open." [20]

Forgiveness moves me out of resignation or fear; connects me to my heart's yearning and what is most meaningful for me, and helps me open up to goodness, energy and vitality in my work and life.

CHAPTER SEVEN

Strengthening Relationships through Forgiveness in Work to Heal the Wounds of War

An essential element to self- forgiveness is often having a safe person one can turn to when it is difficult to shake the voice of inner doubt and criticism. We all, at times, need someone who can hold a mirror up for us when we aren't clearly seeing ourselves. At the end of the talk by JK Rowling which I mentioned earlier, Rowling spoke of the value of her friends. She said, "Failure taught me things about myself that I could have learned no other way. I discovered that I had a strong will, and more discipline than I had suspected; I also found out that I had friends whose value was truly above the rarest rubies."

Parker Palmer says it like this: "Think about a person who helped you grow into some part of your true self, your best self. This was a person who surrounded you with unconditional regard. This person helped you hear a part of your truth and surrounded you with love that said, 'You don't have to be anything different. You are valued and precious as you are.'" [21]

A safe person helps you grow from the inside out. This is in contrast to someone who gives quick advice without really listening, without helping to unravel what you experienced. The opposite of a safe person is someone who will minimize your pain and/or break your confidentiality.

Many of the times that I have found significant self forgiveness, there has been a safe person - a loved one, counselor, coach, friend - who has listened and helped me see my truth self.

Growing a spirit of forgiveness in our lives is expanded exponentially through finding relationships that help us see our true selves. Sometimes this happens through a willingness to stay open, as well as encounters of grace; other times, it takes a great deal of work. Some of the work that helps me develop this in my relationships is staying open to seeing and learning from someone very different from me. Andy Himes describes this so beautifully when he tells a story about an encounter at a veteran's conference in the work he does to help heal the wounds of war through a project called *Voices in Wartime*. Andy had been a war protester at age 19 and realized in hindsight that he had been sure he was right at the time, and that anyone who made a choice to the contrary was morally wrong. But when he realized his errors, he got up on stage and spoke of his error. In response, an ex-marine, Michael, told him that Andy's story had "opened his memory to a story of his own, one he had never told to anyone for 37 years." Michael's memory was about going to a rally as a young active duty soldier with a plan to make a short speech about the importance of stopping hatred. Andy wrote

As Michael was waiting on the platform for his turn to speak, someone saw his uniform and kicked him, driving him off the stage. Michael said he had never before spoken of his shame at being so treated. "You know," he said, "that was more traumatic to me than anything that happened to me in Vietnam in 1968 and 1969."

Andy then continued: After the workshop, Michael said to me, "…You talked about being full of your own sanctified disapproval of soldiers. Nobody's ever apologized to me for what happened that day. And I never knew how much it mattered to me."

Reflecting on the conversation Andy added

Michael told me that our conversation helped him close a chapter of his life in which he had difficulty trusting others or committing himself to being part of a community working for social change. He needed to hear how I had learned I was wrong, how much I wanted and needed to hear his story. …Michael said he needed to experience the liberation that came from forgiving me. For my part, I needed help from Michael to reach across that gap. Somehow that day we both began our lives anew, having reconfigured the gap, having changed each other and ourselves. [22]

What touched me as I read this story is that when Andy named his error and apologized,

it gave Michael an opening to let go and forgive. In turn, Andy's life was renewed in that moment. I wonder if we really ever know how much we need each other. When I back away from my own self-righteousness, safe relationships can develop, sometimes in unexpected ways through grace.

CHAPTER EIGHT

A Little Willingness – Career Derailment

In addition to use of rituals and safe relationships that support forgiveness, there is one more factor I want to mention that has had a profound effect for me. Sometimes when I find myself having the most difficulty forgiving myself it helps me to remember that a first step is just to have a little willingness. Willingness does not need to be big. It can be very tiny, like opening a door just a crack. Willingness happens not by our control, but by opening our hearts. As John Welwood, a well-known psychologist, says, "We cannot heal our alienation from ourselves through some strategy or technique alone. Self-hatred can only be dissolved by taking it to heart." [23]

In some of my most difficult experiences, I find it inconceivable to see how to move toward self forgiveness. But, I have learned that the willingness to forgive starts a natural process. I learned this lesson during one of the most painful times in my life, a time that temporarily derailed my work, career and life. I always knew that Bruce (my best friend and fiancé at the time) was a great teacher in my life, but I didn't expect to learn the lesson in this way. This is my story:

Bruce and I had a fight, and I was unable to stop him from driving away that night in my car. I got a call at three a.m. that my car was totaled, and when I asked what happened to Bruce, I was told he was "in the morgue." I went into a state of shock. And when the sun rose the next morning I couldn't believe it. How could life out there continue as if nothing had happened? My neighbors were getting into their cars and leaving for work and continuing with the motions of life. It all felt alien. I wanted to stop and get off the planet. Grief poured through me, and I felt empty, nauseous, fragile, and weak. How could I understand this tragedy in my life? The roots of my faith were shaken apart. I had to learn to grow and stretch beyond anything I ever imagined. There were moments I simply couldn't function but a kind of grace carried me through the motions of life. Still, I decided I could not continue my private practice as a psychotherapist, even though clients were clearly still having wonderful healing moments and breakthroughs in our sessions. I chose to stop my work, because I questioned whether I had anything to give. I felt completely empty.

The first thing that I remember that helped me was the way Bruce's parents greatly comforted me by reminding me of all that I had meant to them and to Bruce. They told me that Bruce's years with me were the happiest in his entire life. I was comforted, and they opened a door for compassion.

But I still had such deep guilt and pain. I didn't even realize at first that I would need to forgive myself. A survival instinct kicked in. Every instinct in me wanted to run like hell. And those around me tried to help in different ways. Some tried to distract me and told me not to think about things. Several friends told me not to blame myself. One implied that I was in a victim role and needed to quit being a victim. Each piece of advice might have

been helpful. But nothing was
pulling me out of the numbness and
self-deprecation I felt. Someone
gave me the tape cassette
"Subliminal Messages for Letting Go
of Guilt." I never played the tape;
however the word *guilt* reached up
and grabbed me out of my
numbness. "If I'm feeling guilty,
then I need to practice forgiveness,"
I thought to myself. I wasn't sure
how to forgive myself. But
somehow I found myself face to face
with a cycle that was hurting me, and
therefore holding back what I could
give to others. I found a *little
willingness* to self forgive, and that
was the turning point for me.

I did have a journaling process I was
using at the time in which I would
journal my dreams and reflect on
them. My dream work was the ritual
that helped me most. It helped me
to embrace my imperfections, release

my anger, and find a place of peace
inside. One dream I had several
months after Bruce died was a
memorable turning point:

I am with Bruce again. We are back
in time, before his death. I know
that he is going to die. I begin to
think of how I can respond
differently so he will live. When I
find him drunk, I remain very calm
and respond with love. He stands
up to head for the door. Instead of
responding with further blame and
anger, I lovingly tell him I care:
"Please stay." As the dream
progresses, I take every action that I
can think of to do things differently,
to do things right, to be perfect...to
account for any error I thought I had
made. Then suddenly I realize that
in spite of my much more loving
response – even if I respond like a

saint – there is nothing I can do to stop this event. Bruce is going to die. It is not in my power to change it and my actions are inconsequential. Suddenly a weight lifts from my shoulders, almost like being surrounded in light. I can feel all the guilt inside release. I say to Bruce, "If you knew you were going to die, what would you want me to know?" He replies, "I'd want you to think of the image of who I am becoming." I feel a sense of joy that perhaps his soul is living on in some new way.

The peace remained with me as I awoke. It was as if Bruce had reached out and hugged and comforted me.

The dream helped me stop condemning myself and to let go of the unrealistic expectations I had tried to meet. I was imperfect, yes, and I did my best to account for all the things I wish I had done differently. And at the same time, after accounting for my actions in every way I could, after embracing my imperfection, I realized this wasn't about me at all. This was Bruce's life path, and it was between him and his soul. Bruce once told me he felt like he was living on borrowed time. He had expected to die in his 20s. He felt that our years together were a special gift. What I could do now was savor the goodness we shared in the years that we had. I could take the gifts that I received in my relationship with Bruce and carry them with me as I moved forward, as he was doing.

From our relationship I had received many gifts. One was that Bruce had a tremendously open heart. He had taught me to love. I could focus on taking that heightened capacity to love into my current and future relationships. And that is what I did. Six months after this dream, I was filled with new life and joy. A year later I met my husband, Thom. I was back in my work as a psychotherapist in a new setting. I felt I was starting from scratch, but I quickly learned that once I actually got back to the work that called me, I quickly skyrocketed ahead. I moved from being an individual contributor toward leadership work that has been very meaningful. I am grateful for the resilience of life and all that is available to us when we have just a little willingness to forgive, even if we aren't always sure how to forgive ourselves.

I know from this experience and many others that without a doubt, guilt and shame are the wrong direction. When we find ourselves on a slippery slope of suffering and self-criticism, it is imperative that we find a more productive use of our feelings. Then we can begin to move toward that which is life-giving. Like Buckminster Fuller says, we can find that ability to serve life. When we learn to care for ourselves well, we can extend that compassion to others much more powerfully.

Learning to be good to ourselves is not something we do once and then it's done. Martin Luther King Jr. said, "Forgiveness is not an occasional act, it is a permanent attitude." [24]

Every time I go for a great dream, and every time I experience a deep challenge, I encounter expectations that I don't meet. And then I have to find my way to self-forgiveness and self compassion. If I don't, I am not able to really offer compassion to others. Loving ourselves better sometimes means we simply learn to pick ourselves up faster when we have fallen short.

I have found that these thoughts of others

inspire me toward self forgiveness as well:

"When weaving a blanket, an Indian woman leaves a flaw in the weaving of that blanket to let the soul out." Martha Graham

No matter how badly you may be shaken, no matter how serious the failure or how ignominious the fall from grace, by accepting and learning you can be restored with greater strength. Don't lose this basic view of who you are."[25]

Robert Greenleaf

PART 4:

DEFINING MOMENTS: FINDING COURAGE

The stories in this book up to this point have illustrated many workplace challenges for individuals. However, forgiveness also has an impact on teams. Consider what happens when fear is running rampant in a team or organization. Fear can stifle honest conversations. And if teams stay superficial, or if they engage in constant argument and conflict, this drains energy. It is nearly impossible to develop team synergy when the politics of blame or poor ethics are fostered. Most people will not use their greatest creativity when the consequences of mistakes provoke trepidation. Nelson Mandela is quoted as saying that "Forgiveness removes fear and that is why it is so powerful."[26] In this chapter I share one of my own stories of

how forgiveness helped me to find courage
and wisdom to confront a potentially
abusive workplace situation.

CHAPTER NINE

Wisdom in a Potentially Abusive Work Situation

For many years I knew the power of forgiveness in my personal life, but didn't consider applying the same principles that had made such a difference to my home relationships to my workplace.

Here is one of my own examples of a time I was not perfect in my efforts but I faced a defining moment when I had to reach inward to discover who I am at my best.

At the time, I worked for a new boss who appeared to do nothing but try to torpedo my authority as I was learning the ropes of a new job as an agency mid-level manager. I heard from my staff that my boss was speaking in derogatory ways about my every step, and two women reported that he was making inappropriate sexual advances toward them. As I mulled over a confrontation with him, I could think of several ways that any kind of conversation could go very badly. I could become a target or lose my job. However, I was not going to allow this to continue. So, a few days later I found myself sitting across from him at his huge desk. His eyes shifted back and forth; from glaring at me to looking into the distance above his glasses. Our conversation went back and forth, just as his eyes did, resulting in no real communication.

A few days later, I reached out to our CEO for guidance. I was encouraged to try again and "be more direct in the conversation."

My internal dialogue was spinning with questions like, "how can this conversation possibly be any different than it was the last time? I have no reason to trust him."

After a long night, I woke up and realized that the anger and fear I was living in were not serving anyone. I was stuck in a victim story. My mentor, Edith Stauffer, used to say; "How long would you like to continue to carry this burden?" So I asked myself, "How can I be my best self in this situation?" There was no apparent easy answer. But one thing I know to do when tied up in a knot is to use a forgiveness process. I work on getting as calm as I can. Edith would remind me, "There is a place in you where nothing disturbs your peace. With forgiveness you rest in that place." I started by thinking of Edith, since she is a   wisdom figure in my life; someone who is very loving and wise. In a moment I could see the whole thing through her eyes as if I were witnessing it from a mountaintop. I began to breathe a sigh of relief. I could see that I had been expecting and demanding that my boss be supportive of me and our team, but the more I built a case against him, the more entrenched our differences had become. Looking at the situation from a new, more open perspective, the anger began to melt away. I thought of how, in spite of everything, there were still things I valued about my boss. Choosing an attitude of forgiveness meant I let go of my expectations about him and myself, and how this could all resolve. I searched for wisdom. I felt a degree of peace which told me I had made progress in finding a spirit of forgiveness.

Still the next day came and literally my whole body was shaking as I walked back to his office for the meeting. I took some comfort by asking my husband to sit in our workplace lobby just in case anything explosive happened. As I spoke to my boss this time, I found a surprising new strength inside myself. I wasn't cluttered with a victim mentality or a view that he had to change. I stated the challenges as I saw them, as clearly and directly as I could. I skimmed over nothing. And even though he shifted in his chair, I continued, visioning his "best self" as I spoke. I didn't blame him but just gave him examples of what the staff reported and the resulting mixed loyalties and fragmentation I was seeing on the team. Something was different in me as I spoke. I was more firm and clear. He pretty much seemed to ignore what I was saying once again, but I didn't feel so vulnerable in the conversation. I was surprised the very next day to learn that he had been asked to leave the organization. The CEO suddenly saw what was happening and would no longer allow this pattern to continue. I was surprised when several peers arrived in my office wanting to celebrate with champagne. I learned that they had felt oppressed by him for years and years and now they had hope for our organization again.

What I see over and over is that true forgiveness never enables abuse, it only promotes growth. But we can't always predict what healing and growth will look like. A key marker is a sense of peace. Somehow relationships change through forgiveness.

That particular day, a pattern in our organization changed from oppression toward deeper respect, lightness and energy. Yet it wasn't the perfect ending. There was no reconciliation in which my boss and I might have learned from each other and might have been drawn closer together in a healthy form of partnering as leaders enhancing trust in the organization. I don't know if years down the road we will meet and share what we learned.

As a leader, I take my inspiration from the writings of Robert Greenleaf, who emphasizes the importance of always serving the highest priority needs in the way we lead. He says the best test of leadership is "Do those served grow as persons; do they, while being served become healthier, wiser, freer, more autonomous, more likely themselves to

serve? And, what is the effect of the least
privileged in society; will he [or she]
benefit?"[27] Within this situation the best I
could do was serve the highest priority
needs of the team. I would have preferred
not to have had one member cast out.
However, I have learned that sometimes
our paths do take us in different directions
and relationships may end abruptly, and I
have to trust that there is a greater
intelligence than my own in life. With an
attitude of forgiveness, sometimes I get out
of my own way, or I learn to support the
best self and strengths of others rather than
their weaknesses. I do know that
forgiveness will disentangle things; help us
to find wisdom, bring in more grace, and
give us all the opportunity to step into our
best selves.

PART 5:

THE OTHER SIDE OF FORGIVENESS: COURAGE, GENEROSITY AND THRIVING AT WORK

We all face institutional challenges. Some of these have been illustrated in the stories in this book. We face ethical blunders, situations where there is incivility or unkindness, infighting, dysfunctional competition, or when we judge others harshly for their failures, gossip about someone's flaws, and even practice self sabotage. These behaviors become self-reinforcing in a punishing workplace. The opposite of this is to have a workplace culture with the capacities that author and consultant Peter Block writes about, such as "kindness, generosity, cooperation, forgiveness, and the acceptance of fallibility and mystery."[29] These qualities are mutually reinforcing. We become wiser, more generous, more innovative, more collaborative, more peaceful, and more fulfilled when we can let go of unnecessary suffering. Studies of thriving in organizations show that when people feel supported, when they know there is a way to work with their mistakes and flaws, they are buoyed up and will take on challenges and accomplish things they didn't even know they could do.[30] Many thought leaders such as Parker Palmer, Peter Block, Meg Wheatley, Stephen Covey and Ann McGee-Cooper are pointing to the importance of forgiveness more frequently in recent writing. It is a key missing ingredient in working within imperfect systems, for making positive changes on our teams and in our organizations.

But forgiveness is not well understood, and many of us have not had good role models. Robert Cooper, a consultant and expert in emotional intelligence, has observed that "Many of us stubbornly hold onto resentment about life and work because we do not know how to forgive." [30] In one of the following stories, you will read about educators who share their stories of forgiveness and ask important questions about how to grow these skills and use more of their gifts for our children. Also, we will look at a corporate setting where the top leadership fosters apology and forgiveness. Every time true forgiveness happens, I am in awe of what is on the other side.

CHAPTER TEN

Apology and the Ripple Effect at Starbucks Corporation

This is a story about an organization-built from the beginning with the intent to inspire human spirit. Howard Behar told this story at the Greenleaf Conference on Servant leadership in 2009.[31] Howard was a key partner in growing what started as a small Northwest company from 28 stores to more than 400 stores in 47 countries around the world. He explained that from the beginning, part of the mission at Starbucks was, "to be known for nurturing and inspiring human spirit." This forced Howard to think about every action he took and ask himself, "Did this nurture and inspire human spirit?" which is quite a test to ask ourselves each day.

Howard told a story about something that was role modeled for him that connects our ability to care and thrive in our work with a spirit of apology and forgiveness. Here is his unforgettable story:

> About 10 years ago, I got a call at 3am and we had had a catastrophe. Three people were killed in a Starbucks from a bungled robbery; a 24 year old assistant store manager, a 20 year old barista, and a 17 year old barista. Never in my wildest imagination did I ever think that three young people would lose their lives over selling a cup of coffee. I called Howard Schultz and he went right to Georgetown, Washington, D.C. Everything was taped off with yellow lines. No one knew what was happening. The community was shaken. Most CEOs would call their lawyers to ask what to do; or call the PR firm knowing that there could be a huge law suit from this. Not

Howard. Howard got into his rental car and went from home to home to home --visiting each one of the families who lost their children -- crying with them, asking for their forgiveness, accepting responsibility, and asking to do anything he could to help these families.

The first thing that touches me in this story is that it illustrates what is on the other side of forgiveness. The way that Howard Schultz did his best to comfort those families, to help them heal and restore their dignity, showed how one can create caring and connection even in the most painful of circumstances. Experiencing a leader like this, Howard Behar concluded, "Not one time in 20 years did I ever think I couldn't do something caring for another person if that was what was needed, and I knew I would never be questioned -- EVER. ...It is always people first." This has a ripple effect in the organization. Howard Schultz impacted Howard   Behar, and they both likely influenced so many others in the Starbuck's culture. This kind of behavior is contagious.[31]

Also, when I read this story, it gives me an opportunity to ask myself, "What would I have done in Howard Schultz's shoes? Would I have avoided self-protection, fear and guilt, and driven immediately to those families?" I think about what I have done to foster forgiveness and apology, and then all the ways in which I have so much room to grow. Even in my own family, there have been times when I have either witnessed or somehow caused an offense of some kind or a loss of someone's dignity, and I realize that sometimes I take responsibility and apologize, and sometimes I don't. I have lived immersed in habits of self protection, and I have to start where I am and build on every effort I make in the right direction. I try to strengthen my ability to drop unnecessary suffering, to fully accept what is happening in each moment, and to be the change I want to see in my organization – and to do this a little more quickly each time I get off track.

Howard Behar's story reminds me that great leaders are quietly modeling forgiveness and the other virtues that go along with it in ways that become a part of the very fabric of the organizational culture.[32]   These Starbucks corporate leaders have huge financial responsibilities to the stakeholders to whom they are accountable. The work of forgiveness is not about lowering expectations. True forgiveness facilitates excellence. Forgiveness is hardly discussed, sometimes modeled, rarely, if ever, documented as an operating principle or core value. Yet where it is modeled, it operates powerfully.

No organization is perfect, and all of us are

in organizations somewhere on a continuum between highly forgiving, sometimes forgiving, dysfunctional, or punishing. Many of us want to be a part of a positive change in our organizations, families and communities, and in order to do so, we sometimes try to make changes in a reactive way. That usually backfires. Alternatively, we may feel hopeless or cynical and do nothing. But a third alternative is available to us that calls us to be very centered in the midst of a difficulty and to weave caring strands into the culture through our actions. We can create healthy places, little pockets of goodness, even in the midst of a punishing or dysfunctional culture.

Parker Palmer talks about not allowing the dysfunction of an institution to get inside of us and cover over the "imperatives of the heart." The dysfunction of many of our systems does get inside of us easily. I think of one of my own experiences with this. When a company I worked in for years went through a takeover, the organization that came in and made changes was crazy-making. I kept trying to work within the new rules, but I was not able to really use my skills well in an environment that did not encourage creativity. I remember the day my responsibilities were reduced, and I was told I was no longer needed to lead the residential treatment program. I felt shame and deep disappointment, but at the same time as I prepared to leave, I also found myself feeling a strange and unfamiliar sense of peace. I found myself taking time with people and listening to people differently. Looking back, I now realize that the dysfunctional institutional way of being, exhibited by the takeover organization, had indeed gotten inside me; it had replaced my own natural inclination to listen to my heart's imperative. It was very subtle, and it was insidious. Leaving all of that behind released me.

We can all keep learning to get better at staying centered within a difficult or dysfunctional organizational situation. When I find myself in a system that feels punishing, I find it helpful to slow down and ask myself deeper questions, such as"What am I doing or not doing that contributes to the problem?" "How can I live my purpose right where I am?" "Is there any old pattern showing itself here that is familiar from my past or some suffering or pain that keeps recurring?" "Is there anything that could be forgiven and released?" "Is there anything for which I would like to make amends?" "Who am I in this?" Then I do my best to do more listening inside. I break out of my usual routines a little in order to have a little more inner listening time. Simply by asking questions and taking time to listen, major inroads develop. Sometimes I do this through taking time alone, and other times it is through connecting with others

who are committed to this kind of work.
In a recent talk, Daniel Kim[33], a widely
respected systems consultant, urged his
audience to begin changing our
organizational systems in whatever way
might speak to each person. He reminded
us of the deep wisdom in Vaclav Havel's
words, "It is I who must begin ...without
grand speeches ...but rather living
in harmony with the voice inside myself. I
am not the only one. I am not the first one.
I am not the most important one."

In this next chapter, Parker Palmer's story
illustrates how groups with open minds and
hearts can help each other.

CHAPTER ELEVEN

The Heart's Imperative in the Work of Teachers

This story comes from one of the wisest thought leaders I know, Parker Palmer.[34] I have quoted Parker in many chapters throughout this book and I find that I re-read Parker's ideas and stories over and over, year after year, because I learn something new with each reading. In a speech Parker gave at Texas State University, he spoke about a chat room conversation on forgiveness among educators.[35] One teacher had written:

> For years, I have suspected that one of the things that enables good teachers to sustain long careers is their ability to forgive the inevitable disappointments and failures that accompany creative teaching, or any

work for that matter, provide energy, challenge, and stuff to gnaw on only if we aren't gnawed away by them. I want to understand better than I do know how teachers forgive.

Another teacher replied, inspired by the first. She explained that she had been working in a new teaching placement for about eighteen days, and then continued

> I have only just this week realized that my difficulty in a new placement is my lack of forgiveness. I have taught special needs kids for over twenty years, and have just been switched to regular education. I have worked so long with kids who found tasks very difficult, but who worked their hearts out with my encouragement. I now sit looking at able children who barely bother to

show up. I've been furious at them without knowing it, and furious with myself for not being able to make a change.

She added that the "Courage to Teach" chat room conversation had reminded her that

"Expectations become definitions. I have defined their roles in my head and been angry that they have not fulfilled them. I need to forgive, and that has made a difference, but I have room to grow and I welcome suggestions."

There is great truth in the words, *expectations become definitions.* It is so easy to start putting people in boxes, assuming we can't reach them, until we forgive. Peter Block has said, "Our unwillingness to forgive keeps us imprisoned and unable to either offer our gifts or receive the gifts of those around us."[36] I find that to be so true. When I am able to deeply accept flaws in myself and others, I don't hold back my gifts or wait to be perfect. This educator's story reminds me of that truth. How many of us feel it is thankless to serve others who have an attitude of entitlement? And yet the needs of these individuals are just as real; they are just masked. The inner work of releasing unmet demands and expectations, and then looking anew, always brings me new patience and wisdom to find a way through to use my gifts to serve others, rather than holding them back.

One of the many things I value about this online dialogue among educators is that they are asking themselves and each other questions in order to keep growing. Thus, even at a distance, we can see the places in our work where there are opportunities to help each other through our stories, so that we face the *inevitable disappointments and failures*, rather than being *gnawed away by them*. I know these small experiences of unforgiveness can gnaw away at us almost invisibly, and I have seen, alternatively, the amazing energy that develops on the other side of every forgiveness experience.

Here are some quotes I value about the other side of forgiveness:

To forgive is not just to be altruistic, it is the best form of self-interest. …You should never hate yourself for feeling angry. However, when I talk of forgiveness I mean the belief that you can come out the other side a better person. [37] Desmond Tutu

The gift of forgiveness is that we choose not to carry old dysfunctional patterns forward. There is an addition of new emergent positive states of being, most evident in the peace and freedom that develops. Those who learned to forgive become more compassionate and more empowered. The forgiver does not return to baseline, but thrives in becoming forgiving. [38] Mihalache

The primary purpose of leadership is to create an environment of thriving, which allows people to grow, learn and contribute in a safe space where they feel they belong. ...Forgiveness is the most challenging and essential element of attaining a more fulfilling climate at work.[39] Michael Stone.

CHAPTER 12

CLOSING REFLECTIONS

Each time I read a forgiveness story that rings true for me, I learn. I gain a greater understanding of myself and others. And many times I find a deeper or different meaning in a story with a second or third read, or coming back to a story a year later. I find that forgiveness is operating more often than we might think, but often invisibly. Forgiveness has many faces and stories can help us see and understand this powerful possibility in our lives.

The stories in this book illustrate how forgiveness can open the door to:

*Freedom - to change old repeating patterns like a victim story or sense of burden you may be carrying and to let go of self diminishment

*Resilience - to find a sense of harmony in the midst of conflict.

*Courage - to be true to one's best self and develop strength of character

*Relationship - to enhance relationships and experience greater trust and synergy.

*Accomplishment - to see new choices and to let go of self diminishment and put energy into better use.

*Altruism – to serve something deeply important, and to help others.

*Healthier living - to live with greater

physical health and less stress.[40]

I hope that you found at least one story that rang true for you. If you took your thinking further related to your own personal life or workplace possibilities or if something here helped to evoke your own story, that is a great beginning. By sharing our stories we can discover our deeper truths. We can also keep sharing our resources and key insights. And here are some of my current insights:

Choose to forgive

Education about the true meaning of forgiveness can free us to find forgiveness. If someone had not introduced me to what forgiveness really is, I don't know if I would have ever found my way. I grew up thinking forgiveness was more like ignoring, covering over, pretending the pain I felt was not there.

Prepare the way for forgiveness

A key is to start in a state of calm, rather than upset. Practices that help me open my mind and heart help me to start the process of forgiveness.

Start with yourself

It is essential to forgive myself because I will never be perfect in my efforts. It is only by forgiving myself with all my imperfections that I can get better at forgiving others.

Choose to be willing

A key movement in forgiveness is letting go of my old expectations and that requires surrender of control. Edith used to ask,

"How long would you like to continue to carry this burden?" reminding me that this is always a choice if I am willing.

Build on defining moments of forgiveness

Stories about defining moments in our lives teach us a lot. By recognizing defining moments where I chose to forgive, I get better at building on my strengths as a forgiving person, being more true who I am, and letting go of my errors and suffering a little more quickly. And as Angeles Arriene put it, it may be "as if we are in jet lag to who we have become." Hearing the stories of others helps us see more of who we are.

Remember the ripple effect in organizations and communities

We could all use a little more forgiveness in our places of work and in our lives. It has been operating invisibly and may be a missing key to many of the kinds of changes we hope for in our organizations. If we focus on staying centered in difficult organizational or team cross currents we can make small inroads toward more forgiveness in our work lives and communities. I have found that when one heart opens a whole team can change. A spirit of forgiveness can be contagious. At the same time, sometimes efforts will seem fruitless, and it is vital to be patient and to remember that I won't always see the results of the seeds I plant.

I know my learning will be a lifelong endeavor and I expect more insights to develop by sharing more stories. There is a great power in asking ourselves and each other questions, dialogue-style, meaning to take time with questions without rushing to an immediate answer. I would like to end with these questions for you to ask yourself, "What might it take to write a new story for myself? What might it take to write a new story in our organization, to move away from the cynicism and derailment we so often encounter?"   I don't have all the answers to these questions, but I am grateful for what I have learned so far and I look forward to learning more as more stories are shared.

The picture becomes more complete with more stories.   If each of us can inquire in an appreciative manner as to what is working, we can go further. I have listed some resources, further questions for learning, and further stories on my website at www.storiestorenew.com.

ENDNOTES

1. One of the best sources I have found for scholarly research on the benefits of forgiveness can be found at the Fetzer Institute at http://www.forgiving.org/ campaign/research.asp. Collectively the following studies provide information on how forgiveness has the power to enhance health, confidence, happiness, productivity and relationships: Harris, H., Luskin, F., Norman, S., Standard, S., Bruning, J., Evans, S., & Thoresen,C. (2006). Effects of a group forgiveness intervention on forgiveness, perceived stress, and trait-anger. *Journal of Clinical Psychology.* 62. Witvliet, C.V. O., Ludwig, T. E. & Vander Laan, K. L. (2001). Granting forgiveness or harboring grudges: Implications for emotion, physiology, and health. *Psychological Science*, 121, 117-123. Seybold, K.S., Hill, P.C., Neumann, J.K., & Chi, D.S. (2001). Physiological and psychological correlates of forgiveness.

Journal of Psychology and Christianity. 20, 250-259. Berry, J.W., & Worthington, E.L., Jr., (2001). Forgivingness, relationship quality, stress while imagining relationship events, and physical and mental health. *Journal of Counseling Psychology*, 48, 447-455. Sells, J. N., & Hargrave, T. D. (1998). Forgiveness: A review of the theoretical and empirical literature. *Journal of Family Therapy*, 20, 21-36. McCullough, M. E. (2000). Forgiveness as a human strength: Theory, measurement, and links to well-being. Journal of Social and Clinical Psychology, 19(1), 43-55. Bono, G., Mccullough, M. E., & Root, L. M. (2008). Forgiveness, feeling connected to others, and well-being: Two longitudinal studies. *Personality and Social Psychology Bulletin*, 34(2), 182-195.

2. Stone, M. (2002). Forgiveness in the workplace. *Industrial and Commercial Training*, 34(7), 278-286.

3. McGee-Cooper, A. (2009). Unpublished transcription of a session with The Sophia Foundation

Board.

4. This quote was used in Greenleaf's biography by Don Frick and also in an article on forgiveness and servant leadership by Shann Ferch. See both references. Frick, D. M. (2004). *Robert K. Greenleaf: A life of servant leadership.* San Francisco, CA: Berrett-Koehler. Ferch, S. (2011). *Servant-leadership and the Interior of the leader: Facing violence with courage and forgiveness.* In Ferch, S. & Spears, L., *The Spirit of Servant-Leadership.* NY: Paulist Press.

5. The quotes and information from Dr. Fred Luskin are combined from two sources including: Luskin, F. (2002). *Forgive for Good: A Proven Prescription for Health and Happiness.* Harper. Luskin, R. (2003). Conversations with Fred Luskin, PhD. Recorded at the IONS conference called Living Deeply: Expanding Human Capacities. Institute of Noetic Sciences.

6. Notes from Interview with Will Voegele and used with permission.

7. Alice Matzkin's painting of Edith

Stauffer is reprinted from the dual award winning book, *The Art of Aging: Celebrating the Authentic Aging Self*, Boulder, CO: Sentient Publications, 2009. Copyright © 2009 by Richard and Alice Matzkin. Used by permission of Sentient Publications and Alice Matzkin.

8. Stauffer, E. (1987). *Unconditional Love and Forgiveness.* Diamond Springs, CA: Triangle Publishers. Quoted with permission of Edith's daughter, Barbara Giles.

9. Luskin, ibid.

10. Childre, D. L. & Martin, H. (2000). *The HeartMath Solution: The Institute of HeartMath's Revolutionary Program for Engaging the Power of the Heart's Intelligence.* HarperOne.

11. From a Gallup study as quoted in Gorsuch, R. L. & Hao, J. Y. Forgiveness: An exploratory factor analysis and its relationship to religious variables, *Review of Religious Research.* 34 (4) 351-363.

12. Frankl, V. (1993). *Man's search for meaning.* Buccaneer Books.

13. Luskin ibid.

14. Stauffer ibid.

15. The story of Buckminster Fuller was first told to me by a friend. I confirmed the story and learned even more through The Buckminster Fuller Institute at http://www.bfi.org/

16. J. K Rowling, J.K. (2008). _Commencement: The Fringe Benefits of Failure, and the Importance of Imagination._ Keynote speech. Retrieved from http://harvardmagazine.com/2008/06/the-fringe-benefits-failure-the-importance-imagination

17. Taft, L. (2000). Apology Subverted: The Commodification of Apology. _Yale Law Journal._ Yale Law Journal Company.

18. Rutledge, T. (1997). _The Self forgiveness handbook._ New Harbinger Publications.

19. Note that there are many great books that provide forgiveness processes with steps such as Stauffer, E. (1987). _Unconditional Love and Forgiveness._ Diamond Springs, CA: Triangle Publishers. Luskin, F. (2002). _Forgive for Good: A Proven Prescription for_

Health and Happiness. Harper., Enright, R. (2001). *Forgiveness Is a Choice: A Step-By-Step Process for Resolving Anger and Restoring Hope.* American Psychological Association. And The Fetzer Institute's Campaign for Unconditional Love and Forgiveness has a variety of forgiveness practices at website: http://www.fetzer.org/loveandforgive/take-action/practice-love-a-forgiveness. For a growing list of sources and a way to use stories to enhance forgiveness practices see www.storiestorenew.com

20. Martha Graham is quoted by Agnes De Mille who is author of the biography; De Mille, Agnes (1992). *Martha: The Life and Work of Martha Graham.* New York: Vintage Books.

21. Palmer, P. (2009). *A Hidden Wholeness: The Journey Toward an Undivided Life.* San Francisco: Jossey-Bass. p 59-62

22. Himes, A. (2005). *Voices in Wartime: The Anthology.* Whit Press.

23. Welwood, J. (2000). *Toward a psychology of awakening.* Boston, MA:

Shambhala Publications.

24. King, C.S. (2008). *The words of Martin Luther King.* Newmarket Press.

25. Greenleaf in McGee-Cooper, A. & Trammel, D. (1998). *Awakening Sleeping Genius: A Journaling Approach to Personal Grown and Servant-Leadership.* Dallas, TX: AMCA, Inc.

26. Eastwood, C. [Director, Producer]. (2009). *Invictus.* Motion Picture. Warner Brothers Studios.

27. Greenleaf, R. (1977). *The Servant as Leader.* Indianapolis: The Greenleaf Center for Servant Leadership

28. McKnight, J. & Block, P. (2010). The *Abundant Community: Awakening the Power of Neighborhoods and Communities.* Berrett-Koehler Publishers.

29. There are a variety of studies of thriving from the field of Positive Psychology. See for example, Jenkins, P. (2010). *A case study of collective thriving at work.* Capella University. UMI Dissertations International. Spreitzer, G., Sutcliffe, K., Dutton, J., Sonenshein, S., & Grant, A. M. (2005). A socially embedded model of thriving at work. *Organization*

Science, 16(5), 537-549. Carmeli, A., & Gittell, J. H. (2009). High-quality relationships, psychological safety, and learning from failures in work organizations. *Journal of Organizational Behavior*. 30, 709-729.

30. Cooper, R & Sawaf, A. (1998) *Executive E.Q.* Perigee Trade.

31. Behar, H. (personal communication, 2009). Keynote speech at the Greenleaf Conference on Servant Leadership.

32. There are a variety of articles on forgiveness in the workplace and the impact on relationships and culture. See for example: Aquino, K., Grover, S. L., Goldman, B., & Folger, R. (2003). When push doesn't come to shove: Interpersonal forgiveness in workplace relationships. *Journal of Management Inquiry*, 12(3), 209-216. Madsen, S. Gygi, J., Hammond, S., Plowman, S. (2009). *A forgiving workplace: An investigation of forgiveness climate, individual differences and workplace outcomes.* Journal of Behavioral & Applied Management. 10 (2). 246-

262. Cox, S. Louisiana Tech University, 2008. Cameron, K., & Caza, A. (2002). Organizational and leadership virtues and the role of forgiveness. *Journal of Leadership & Organizational Studies*, 9(1), 33-48.

33. Kim, D. (personal communication, June, 2011). Keynote speech at the Greenleaf Center for Servant Leadership Conference.

34. One example of the wisdom of Parker Palmer is found in the book which celebrates his life and work: Intrator, S. (2005). *Living the Questions: Essays Inspired by the Work and Life of Parker J. Palmer.* San Francisco, CA: Jossey-Bass.

35. Parker, P. (2003). Unpublished keynote speech at the University of Texas. LBJ Distinguished Lecture. Retrieved from http://www.txstate.edu/commonexperience/pastsitearchives/2008-2009/lbjresources/lbjlectures/contentParagraph/0110/document/2003-04-28-palmer.pdf.

36. McKnight & Block, ibid.

37. Desmond Tutu as quoted at http://www.theforgivenessproject.c

om/stories/leatitia

38. *Mihalache, G.* (2008). *Transformational forgiveness: A heuristic study of the self-transforming nature of becoming forgiving following traumatic events.* UMI Dissertations International.

39. Stone, M. (2002). Forgiveness in the workplace. *Industrial and Commercial Training, 34*(6/7), 278-286.

40. A few of the many studies that correlate forgiveness and health include: Witvliet, C.V. O., Ludwig, T. E. & Vander Laan, K. L. (2001). Granting forgiveness or harboring grudges: Implications for emotion, physiology, and health. *Psychological Science*, 121, 117-123. Seybold, K.S., Hill, P.C., Neumann, J.K., & Chi, D.S. (2001). Physiological and psychological correlates of forgiveness. *Journal of Psychology and Christianity.* 20, 250-259.

ABOUT THE AUTHOR

Deborah Welch, Ph.D. coaches leaders in colleges, school districts, foundations, corporations and small businesses.

She has been a faculty member at Capella University since 1999 teaching graduate level courses in the psychology of leadership and guiding dissertation work.

She is an innovator in virtual learning processes for support and learning across distances. She designed and has co-facilitated a year long peer leadership coaching program with experts Ann McGee-Cooper and Virginia Gilmore since 2007.

Deborah studied with Dr. Edith Stauffer, a globally known educator on forgiveness for 50 years whose book on the topic has been translated into 11 languages.

Deborah finds that the use of stories are a

powerful way for us to take our practices further. She continues to be inspired by her clients as to the amazing power of forgiveness. And she is a life long student personally practicing to continually learn the gift of forgiveness for thriving in work and life.

OTHER WORKS

by DEBORAH WELCH Ph.D.

❖ Coaching for Servant-Leadership. A chapter in The Spirit of Servant Leadership, edited by Ferch and Spears. (available at Amazon.com)

❖ Reflective Leadership: The Stories of Five Leaders Successfully Building Generative Organizational Culture, Dissertation available at www.Reflective-Leadership.com

❖ Thriving at Work Through Forgiveness an article in www.dynamiclivingmagazine.com, May 2011 issue.

❖ Transforming Leadership: The Story of Robert Greenleaf an article published in The Systems Thinker

❖ For more stories and resources on forgiveness and renewal visit www.storiestorenew.com

Notes

Notes

Notes

Notes

Made in the USA
Charleston, SC
09 November 2011